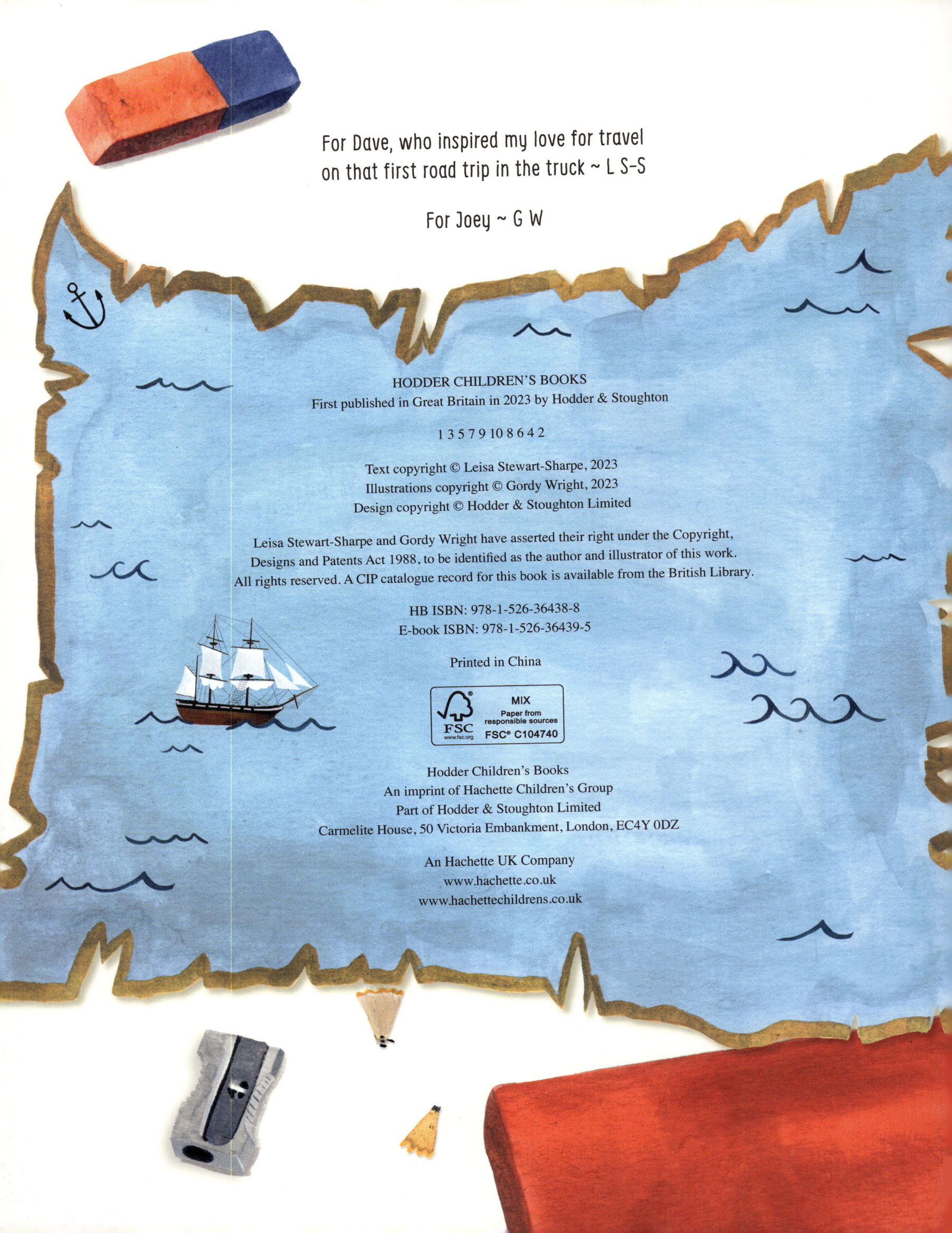

For Dave, who inspired my love for travel
on that first road trip in the truck ~ L S-S

For Joey ~ G W

HODDER CHILDREN'S BOOKS
First published in Great Britain in 2023 by Hodder & Stoughton

1 3 5 7 9 10 8 6 4 2

Text copyright © Leisa Stewart-Sharpe, 2023
Illustrations copyright © Gordy Wright, 2023
Design copyright © Hodder & Stoughton Limited

Leisa Stewart-Sharpe and Gordy Wright have asserted their right under the Copyright,
Designs and Patents Act 1988, to be identified as the author and illustrator of this work.
All rights reserved. A CIP catalogue record for this book is available from the British Library.

HB ISBN: 978-1-526-36438-8
E-book ISBN: 978-1-526-36439-5

Printed in China

MIX
Paper from
responsible sources
FSC® C104740

Hodder Children's Books
An imprint of Hachette Children's Group
Part of Hodder & Stoughton Limited
Carmelite House, 50 Victoria Embankment, London, EC4Y 0DZ

An Hachette UK Company
www.hachette.co.uk
www.hachettechildrens.co.uk

THE TREASURE HUNT

True stories of treasures
LOST, STOLEN and **FOUND**

LEISA STEWART-SHARPE

Illustrated by
GORDY WRIGHT

Hodder
Children's
Books

X MARKS THE SPOT

. . . or does it?

Let's be sensible, if you were a pirate, and you'd gone to all the trouble of stashing your hoard, you're hardly going to give away its hiding place with a great big X on the map, are you?

Then again, maybe you're a *forgetful* pirate, the kind who loses his reading glasses or her keys, in which case an X on the map begins to make more sense.

The one thing we can be sure of is that pirates really did have treasure...

PILES OF IT.

Treasure hunters are still searching for it today, as well as scouring the globe for:

- modern masterpieces
- ancient ruins
- priceless jewels
- archaeological artefacts.

While many treasures lost to time or stolen have been found, plenty more are waiting to be discovered.

So, switch on your metal detector and grab your compass. It's time for YOU to do some treasure hunting of your own to discover if X really does mark the spot.

This is YOUR treasure hunt, and YOU get to be a...

cartographer (map reader)

cryptologist (code cracker)

enigmatologist (puzzle solver)

epigrapher (ancient inscriptions decipherer)

You'll need some blank paper and a pencil. If you want to solve a clue for yourself, don't turn the page, otherwise you'll see the answer. If you get stuck, there are HINTS (and some answers!) on pages 56–61. Your treasure hunt begins...

NOW!

A SECRET FROM THE SEA...

Your story begins with you huddled around a beach campfire next to your best friends Saksham and Zuri. The three of you share everything — secrets, socks and especially stories. And nobody tells them better than you! They're just the right amount of spooky and full to the brim with...

PIRATES!

You lean in, casting a shadow over your friends' eager faces...

'It begins, in the dead of night and the heart of the storm!'

A huge wave pounds the shore, making everyone *jump!*

As the clouds creep past the moon, something twinkles on the sand.
It's a bottle; green and slippery with algae. Zuri pulls out the cork, and a
scroll of soggy paper slides into her hand. The colour drains from your face...

                        it's sealed with a **SKULL**.

                    Zuri unfurls the paper and begins to read:

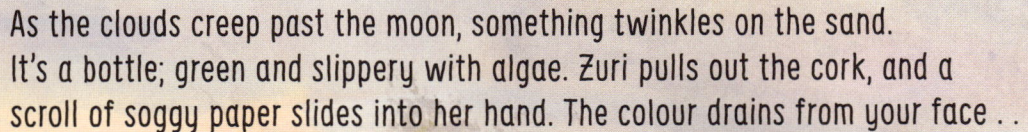

*I stare into the silver sea,
what treasure do you hide from me?
I search each street and castle keep,
my dreams glow gold in darkest sleep.
I'll find them all – ne'er walk the plank
then like the Galley, they'll be sank
beneath that deepest silver sea.
Their resting place? Unknown to thee.*

Captain Kidd

Surely not **the Captain Kidd**, notorious Scottish pirate?
Legend has it he buried treasure all over the world. But what could
this poem mean? What is he searching for? Maybe there's a clue in
one of your books back home...

THE TALE OF CAPTAIN KIDD

Shiver me timbers, it's the 1690s and the high seas are riddled with pirates!

They're stealing everything.

And England is fed up.

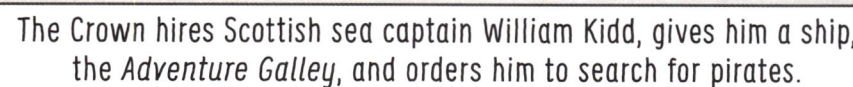

The Crown hires Scottish sea captain William Kidd, gives him a ship, the *Adventure Galley*, and orders him to search for pirates.

Kidd isn't very good at it!

After two years, Kidd's crew force him to become a pirate and capture the *Quedagh Merchant*!

Kidd sinks the leaky *Adventure Galley* and sets sail on the stolen ship . . .

. . . only to be arrested . . .

. . . and hanged for piracy in 1701.

He had to be hanged TWICE (the rope broke the first time!)

But whatever came of the *Quedagh Merchant's* treasure? Some believe Kidd stashed it on the *Adventure Galley* before it sank, and that it's on the ocean floor, waiting to be found.

And that's when you spot a newspaper on the table.

DAILY NEWS

'PIRATE GHOST' destroys priceless fresco!

The art world was left shaken last night after *The Battle of Marciano* fresco in Florence, Italy, was vandalised by a mysterious figure. Historians believe he was looking for Leonardo da Vinci's unfinished mural *The Battle of Anghiari* that some think is hidden in a cavity behind a huge fresco by Giorgio Vasari.

CCTV footage from inside the Palazzo Vecchio shows the culprit used a sledgehammer to smash a hole in the fresco. He was disturbed by security, then, like a ghost, vanished into the night.

Museum Curator Francesca De Luca says: 'The man was wearing a pirate costume, as though it was all a great joke to him. Well, we're certainly not laughing.'

The search continues.

By Giana Magaddino

First, a letter from Captain Kidd, then news that a ghostly pirate has tried to steal a missing da Vinci. Is the ghost of Captain Kidd planning to steal all the world's treasures as revenge for the riches he lost all those years ago?

Luckily, nobody reads a map like Saksham, you're a master code cracker and armed with her history book, Zuri is unstoppable! If anyone can track down a treasure-thieving ghost pirate, it's the three of you! You search online and find out that a ship leaves for **Italy** in the morning, and you plan to be on it!

HISTORY OF FLORENCE

In the fifteenth century, the Palazzo Vecchio was home to the powerful Medici family. They lavished their vast fortune on commissioning paintings and sculptures that helped the careers of the great Renaissance artists, including . . .

Botticelli

da Vinci

Michelangelo

Raphael

The 54-metre-long Hall of Five Hundred got its name from the 500-man Grand Council that met here before the Medici family moved in. The chamber walls are painted with the enormous *The Battle of Marciano* fresco, but before the artist Giorgio Vasari painted this, Leonardo da Vinci was commissioned to paint *The Battle of Anghiari* mural. Unhappy with his work, Leonardo abandoned it and the mural was believed lost.

FRESCO FIASCO

After your long journey, it feels good to stretch your legs as you weave through **Florence's** bustling Piazza della Signoria. You're in the heart of the city, flanked by the Fountain of Neptune and overlooked by a medieval palace called **Palazzo Vecchio**. But there's no time for sightseeing — you have a Ghost Captain to find!

You pass a replica statue of Michelangelo's *David* as you enter the palace . . .

. . . and climb the stairs to the Hall of Five Hundred.

WHEN MASTERPIECES GO MISSING

'I've got it!' you shout! The symbols spell *Le Musée du Louvre*. That's an art museum in **Paris**, France – one very long bus ride away...

On the bus, Saksham turns on his tablet and types in 'missing art', searching for a clue to what the Ghost Captain is up to. Before long, you're all spellbound by stories of famous art heists.

'GENTLEMEN, THIS IS A ROBBERY!'

... these are the words two men announced as they entered the Isabella Stewart Gardner Museum in Boston, USA, one morning in 1990. Dressed as police officers, they tied up the guards and set to work cutting paintings from their frames. The thieves stole into the night with 13 treasured artworks by Rembrandt, Vermeer, Degas and Manet worth around £400 million. Neither the thieves or the art were seen again.

CASE UNSOLVED

THE TAKEAWAY REMBRANDT

Rembrandt's 1632 painting *Jacob de Gheyn III* has been stolen and recovered not once, not twice, but four times from a picture gallery in London, UK. In fact, Rembrandt's works have been stolen more than 80 times from galleries around the world.

CASE SOLVED

STOLEN IN 50 SECONDS

In 1994, two thieves broke through a window of the National Gallery in Oslo, Norway. They stole Edvard Munch's painting *The Scream*, worth more than £99 million, but not before they left the note: 'Thousand thanks for the poor security!' For all their confidence, the painting was found in a hotel and the thieves eventually caught.

CASE SOLVED ✓

NEVER TO BE SEEN AGAIN . . .

On a stormy night in 1969, Caravaggio's £16 million *Nativity with St Francis and St Lawrence* was stolen from the wall of a church in Palermo, Italy.

CASE UNSOLVED ✗

THE 'LOOVRE'

In 2003, artworks by Gauguin, Picasso and Van Gogh worth around £4 million were stolen from a gallery in Manchester, UK. They were stuffed into a cardboard tube and stashed in a run-down toilet block, later given the nickname 'the Loovre'. When found, the tube held a message: 'The intention was not to steal, only to highlight the woeful security.'

CASE SOLVED ✓

FLOWER THEFT

Twice stolen from Cairo, Egypt, Van Gogh's £45 million *Poppy Flowers* is still at large, as is the thief who took it.

CASE UNSOLVED ✗

13

THE FRENCH JOB

It's midnight as you and your friends run through the streets of **Paris**. The world's largest art museum comes into view — Le Musée du Louvre. The next thing you notice is the wailing of sirens.

Someone has set off the alarms.

That someone **must** be the Ghost Captain!

'What do you think he's trying to steal?' Saksham puffs as he runs beside you.

Of all the museum's precious artworks, one painting comes to mind... the **Mona Lisa**.

And it wouldn't be the first time someone tried to steal her...

～ HISTORY OF THE WORLD ～
MONA WENT MISSING

In 1911, Vincenzo Peruggia walked into the Louvre, headed to the Salon Carré where the *Mona Lisa* hung, squeezed into a closet and went to sleep.

The next morning, he took the *Mona Lisa* from her frame, slipped her under his coat and walked out.

For two years, an army of detectives failed to find the stolen painting.

In 1913, with Mona tucked inside a false-bottom trunk, Peruggia travelled to Florence.

He tried to sell her to an art dealer, who convinced Peruggia to leave Mona with him for inspection.

The dealer alerted the police and Peruggia was arrested.

The *Mona Lisa* is now one of the world's most famous paintings.

In all the commotion, you slip into the museum through the crowd, and sprint towards its biggest room, the Salle des États. Here, Mona smiles down at you from inside her temperature- and humidity-controlled glass box.

'That's bulletproof glass,' Zuri whispers. 'And look, the cameras and guards are always watching.'

A little later, when the crowds have been asked to leave, you overhear a guard describing what happened . . .

This guy comes from nowhere, vaults over the barrier and spray paints the glass! I set off the alarms and he took off through the fire exit.

What could those letters and numbers mean?

CLUE

Unknot these numbers using the prompts on p. 56.

✼ HISTORY OF MOSCOW ✼

In Russian, 'kremlin' means fortress – buildings once used to defend cities from invaders. Moscow's 500-year-old Kremlin is perhaps the most famous of all. It was once a palace for the Russian emperors (Tsars). It has 20 towers, secret passageways, churches, cathedrals and a huge armoury chamber holding countless treasures, including priceless Fabergé eggs.

For more than three centuries from 1547, Russia was ruled by the Tsars. The last royal family were known as the Romanovs, and their palaces in and around Saint Petersburg overflowed with treasures, including the Imperial crown jewels. But in 1917, starving workers began to riot in the streets, ultimately overthrowing the monarchy. This was known as the Russian Revolution and was led by the revolutionary Vladimir Lenin. The Romanovs' treasures were sent to the Kremlin armoury for safekeeping, although many have disappeared over the years.

An UnEGGSPECTED CLUE

'They're map coordinates!' Saksham shouts. His fingers follow the numbered lines on the map and meet over your next destination – **Moscow**, Russia. Let's go!

After one of the world's longest train rides, you make your way across Moscow's Red Square, where snow dusts the brightly coloured domes of Saint Basil's Cathedral. Towering before you are the red-bricked walls of the Kremlin.

Suddenly, sirens begin to *wail*.

'Look!' Saksham shouts. A cloaked figure has thrown open a side door of the Kremlin and is shoving their way through the crowd, clutching something shiny in their hands. You run towards them but get caught up in the throng of woolly coats.

'Ow!' you exclaim as somebody steps on your toes. You look down at your feet — something is sparkling in the snow . . .

It's a Fabergé egg!

This must be what the Ghost Captain stole from inside and rather than get caught red-handed, he's tossed it away like rubbish. You cradle the egg in one hand, running your fingers over the glittering gems.

Click . . .

it pops open. **There's something inside!**

Saksham pulls out a long piece of paper. But the word written on it makes no sense:

HARTENSTEIN

CLUE

Go to p. 56 for a hint on how to crack the code.

THE MYSTERY OF THE TSARS' TREASURES

You stare at the word and soon realise . . . it's written backwards!
HARTENSTEIN. Could that be a place? Quick, check the map on pages 62–63.

Hartenstein is a small town in Germany — where the Ghost Captain plans to strike again!

On the train, Zuri opens her history book to find out more about the Romanovs' missing treasures.

HISTORY OF THE WORLD

ALL ABOARD THE TREASURE TRAIN!

In 1918, it's believed piles of the Romanovs' gold were loaded on to an armoured 'treasure train' to flee the Bolshevik army in Saint Petersburg. According to some stories, the train escaped Lenin's Red Army only to get captured by Czech forces, who stashed the gold on their own overloaded train. But as it skirted around the edge of the world's deepest lake, Lake Baikal, could its wheels have lost traction? Did the train tip and become swallowed by the lake for good? Locals still search the lake's freezing depths for the lost gold today.

THE LOST LIBRARY

Never mind losing your library card . . . imagine losing an entire library! According to legend, in the sixteenth century, Ivan IV (known as Ivan the Terrible) inherited the family library. It held rare manuscripts and literary masterpieces from around the world. Some say Ivan hid the library before his death, and the books were never seen again.

HISTORY OF THE WORLD
EASTER SURPRISE!

1885

Tsar Alexander III asked jeweller Peter Carl Fabergé to create a fancy Easter gift for his wife.

It looked like an egg, but inside was . . . a gold yolk.

And inside the yolk was . . . a gold hen. Surprise!

And inside the hen . . . there were jewels!

The Empress was delighted and Fabergé eggs became a royal Easter tradition.

Fifty eggs were created for the Romanovs. They were *full* of surprises.

1917

After the Russian Revolution, the eggs were sold around the world. Many are still missing!

2014

One day in the USA, a man bought an egg at a flea market. 'Bargain! I could sell it as scrap metal!' he thought.

Far from 'scrap' . . . it was the long-lost Third Imperial Fabergé Egg!

THE CASE OF THE MISSING ROOM

Several train rides later, you roll into the pretty German town of . . .

Hartenstein

Before long, you're munching on a salty pretzel as you marvel at the pointy spires of the town's medieval castle.

The villagers are excitedly chatting, as treasure hunters think they've found Russia's missing **Amber Room** outside of town. Is this what the Ghost Captain's looking for?

～～ HISTORY OF THE WORLD ～～

THE AMBER ROOM

Imagine a room made from amber panels, gold leaf and jewels! Once the crowning glory of Catherine Palace near Saint Petersburg in Russia, the Amber Room disappeared during the Second World War, when Hitler invaded Russia. The Romanovs desperately tried to hide it under wallpaper so it wouldn't be stolen. But the German Nazi soldiers found it, took it apart and reinstalled it in Königsberg Castle in Germany, which was later bombed. Was the Amber Room still inside or had it already been moved to a new secret location?

Zuri's history book shares a few theories. It says some people think the Amber Room is hiding in a sunken warship, a railway tunnel or . . . deep inside Hartenstein's hills, where you spot a crowd gathering at the mouth of a cave.

Treasure hunters are looking at radar images that suggest a network of secret tunnels wind under the hill. And there's evidence that crates may have been lowered inside.

You ask the treasure hunters if they've seen a pirate ghost snooping around, only to be met with laughter. You fix your gaze on a rock to stop yourself from blushing and that's when you spot something . . .

It looks like scratches, but on closer inspection, you see the rock face is etched with dots and dashes. Could it be a message from the Ghost Captain in **Morse code?**

CLUE

To crack the code, go to p. 57.

21

○ HISTORY OF NORWAY ○

From around the ninth century, Vikings travelled across Europe. The seafaring warriors from the countries now known as Norway, Denmark and Sweden would attack and raid settlements, taking whatever treasures they could carry! In the Vikings' own stories, treasure hoards were guarded from thieves by fire-breathing dragons, but in reality, they were often buried.

Vikings didn't just raid, they'd also trade. High up on the Lendbreen mountain pass, in the heart of Norway, archaeologists have found a treasure trove of fascinating artefacts.

TREASURE UNDER THE ICE

Dots and dashes swim before your eyes as you decode the message. It says: Lendbreen Mountain Pass. You scan the map and spot **Lendbreen** is in Norway. That must be where the Ghost Captain has gone next — let's go!

You catch a number of buses and trains through Germany, then board a ferry to Norway. After docking in the capital of Oslo, you take a bus and then finish the last part of the journey on foot, as the hike to the Lendbreen ice patch is strenuous, some 1,900 metres high.

Once home to the Vikings, perhaps the Ghost Captain is searching for some buried Viking treasure?

As the world has become warmer, the ice on top of this mountain has melted, revealing a perfectly preserved 1,700-year-old woollen tunic, woollen mittens, leather shoes, hunting tools, horse bones and even piles of horse poo!

They tell archaeologists that Vikings used this trail, marked by a line of cairns (stone piles), to move cattle to summer pastures or as a trade route.

But what's that?

Rocks from a nearby cairn have been arranged in the snow.

Zuri's eyes gleam with excitement. 'From over here, those stones look a lot like **Nordic runes** — that's an ancient alphabet!'

CLUE

Use the archaeologist's notebook on p. 57 to decipher the runes.

HOARDS UNLOCKING HISTORY

The runes read: *natiǫnal musium ǫf skǫtlant*. 'When you say it aloud, it sounds like the National Museum of **Scotland!**' Zuri exclaims.

In the late eighth century, Vikings set sail across open waters, travelling far and wide. Now you will too! But before you leave Norway, there's something you must see in one of Oslo's museums . . .

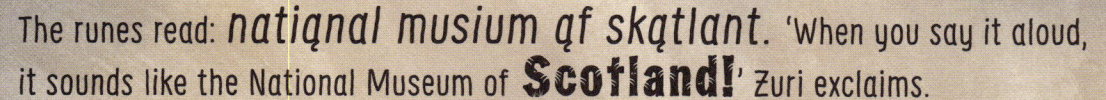

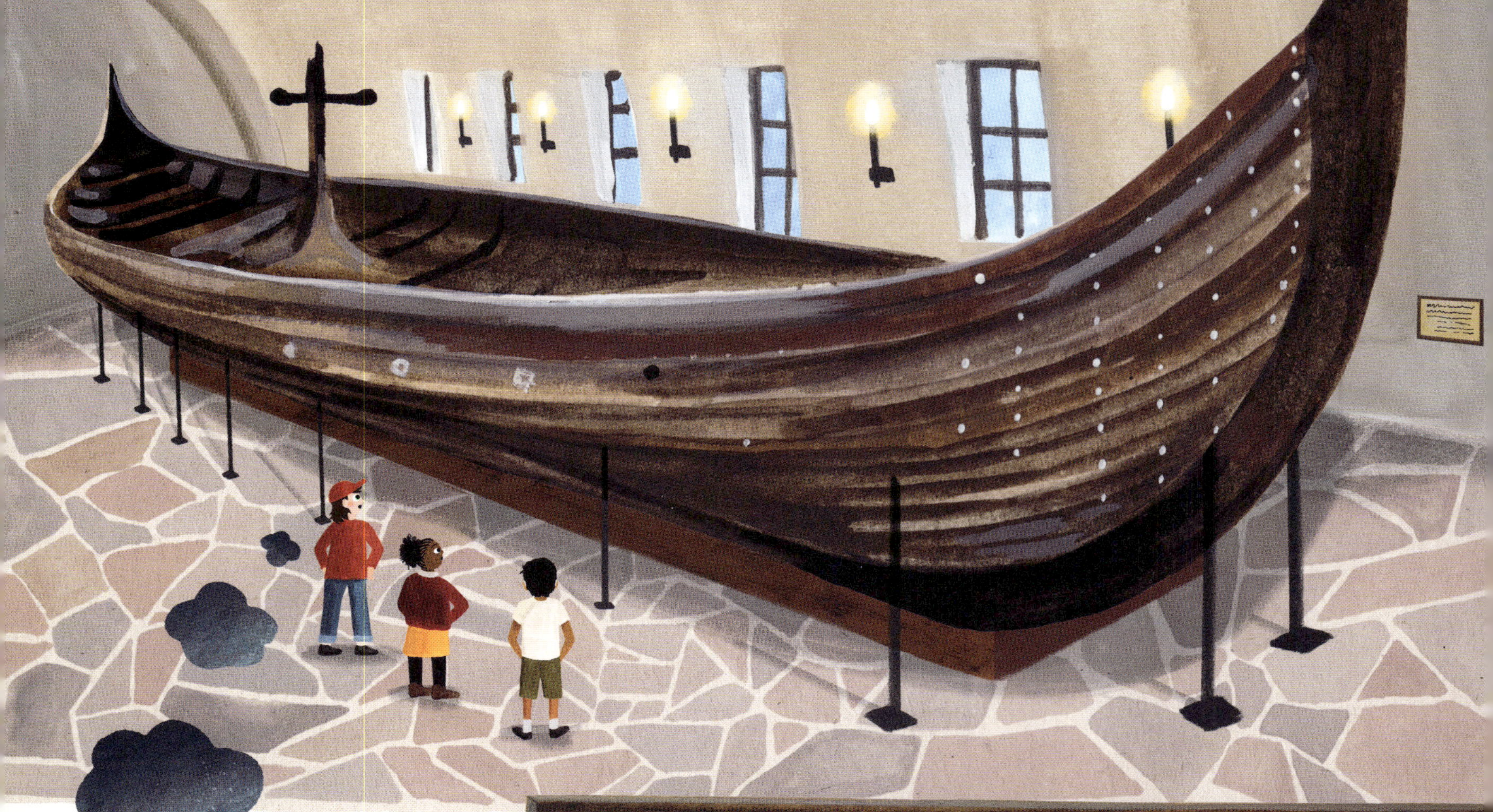

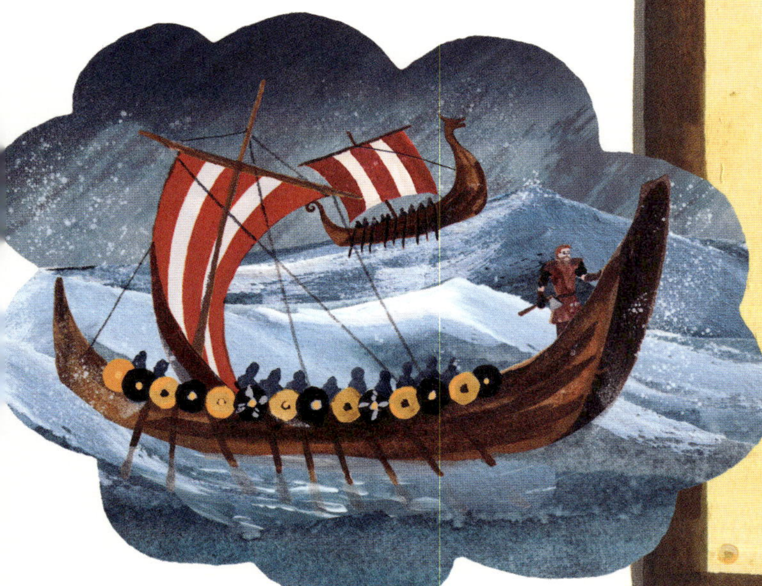

Imagine the terror of seeing the *Gokstad* ship bearing down on your village. Built around 890 CE, for years it was believed to be the stuff of legends. Then, in 1879, two determined boys began digging in the grounds of their farm in Oslofjord. Before long, and with the help of an archaeologist, the 23-metre-long Viking ship *Gokstad* was unearthed.

Part of a burial mound, the ship had been underground for almost 1,000 years. As well as retaining much of its original wood, it held a man's skeleton, surrounded by the bones of dogs, horses and even a peacock. It was a burial chamber fit for a king.

The museum curator loans you her research folder for the boat ride to Scotland. Perhaps you'll find a clue to what the Ghost Captain's looking for?

HANDS OFF THAT HOARD!

In 2015, four men tried to keep a valuable Viking hoard a secret and three went to jail for it! The 1,000-year-old hoard was dug up in an English field, and included jewellery, silver ingots (bars used by the Vikings as currency) and coins. While some of the hoard has been recovered, many coins are still missing. Historians believe a single Viking penny could be worth thousands of pounds, which drove one antique dealer to hide them inside the handle of his magnifying glass!

WOMEN WARRIORS

In 1878, archaeologists discovered an ornate tomb in the Swedish Viking town of Birka. It contained horses, a full set of weapons and games used to plan military attacks. It was the tomb of a great warrior. Almost 140 years later, DNA testing has revealed that warrior was a woman; an insight into women's high-ranking status in Viking society.

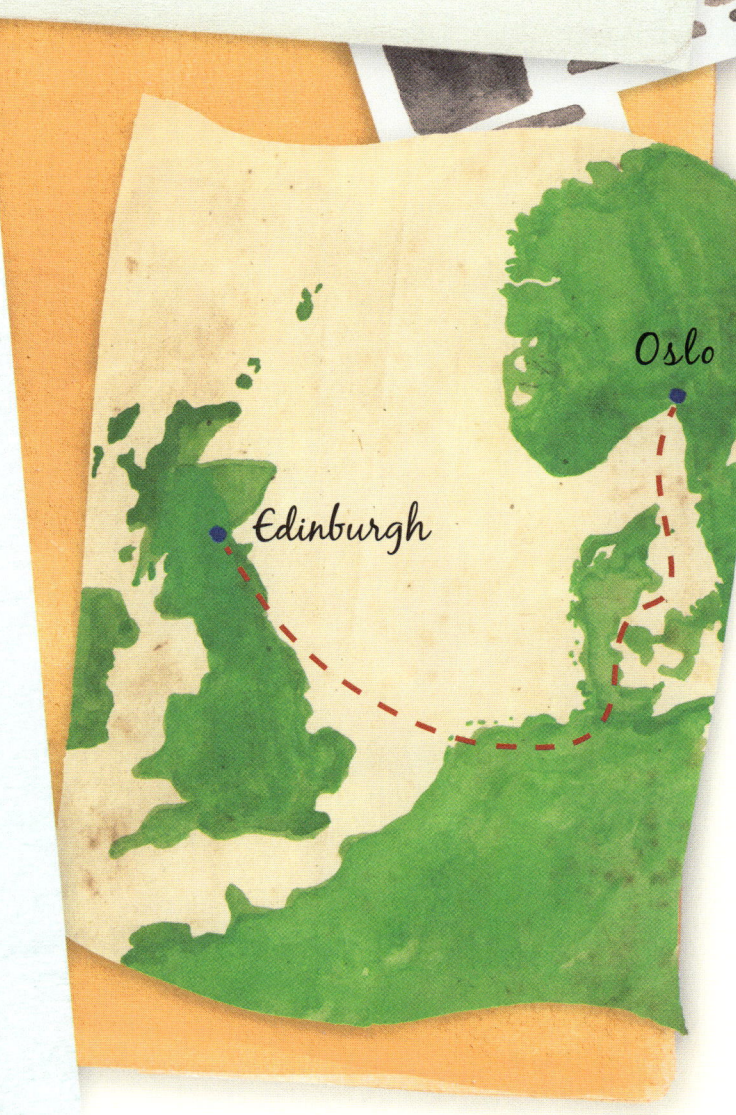

CHECKMATE!

You arrive in the Scottish capital, **Edinburgh**. Its gothic skyline is crowned by Edinburgh Castle, perched atop an extinct volcano. Nearby is the National Museum of Scotland, which is where your taxi is headed now. You made good time on the crossing from Norway — time to catch the Captain!

As you and your friends dash into the museum, a huge banner hangs across the vaulted great hall . . .

LEWIS CHESS PIECES - LEVEL 1

'That's got to be it!' Saksham shouts. 'Quick guys, find the stairs!'

VIKING BOARD GAMES

The Vikings loved a board game, especially chess. In 1831, on the Scottish Isle of Lewis, 93 chess pieces were found buried on a beach. Elaborately carved from walrus tusks or whale teeth, they became known as the Lewis Chessmen, used by Norse Vikings in the twelfth and thirteenth centuries. Archaeologists believed the pieces came from four different chess sets, which meant many were still missing, including one knight, four warders (rooks) and 44 pawns! The mystery of one of those warders was solved in 2019 when a Lewis Chessman emerged from a grandfather's drawer, where it had lain for 55 years.

Eager to lay eyes on the chessmen, you take the stairs two at a time.

But as you go up, someone in a cloak rudely shoulders past you on the way down.

There's no time to dwell on it . . . you've arrived at level one. As you run over to the Lewis Chessmen display, you notice the curator scratching her head.

'How mysterious,' she says. 'Someone's left a note!'

On seeing the tight security, the Ghost Captain must have realised it would be impossible to steal the Chessmen. Instead, he taped a **riddle** to the glass. Can you solve it?

I lie in a **Valley** in Egypt's heat,
the heart **of the** hills that does not beat.
Kings and their Queens in lasting sleep,
surrounded by treasures we longed to keep.
Where am I?

CLUE

Need help unravelling the riddle? Go to p. 58.

27

HISTORY OF LUXOR

Around 1500 BCE, rather than being buried in pyramids, the pharaohs of Egypt's New Kingdom were buried in elaborate, underground tombs dug into the Theban Hills. Each tomb was a lavish final resting place for pharaohs, queens, high priests and other important people. First, the pharaohs were mummified, a process used to preserve their bodies, as they believed their soul could come alive again in the afterlife. Then, they were put inside a sarcophagus – a stone container that held the coffin. The tomb held everything they might need in the afterlife, including jewellery, furniture, food and even pets.

Most of the hidden tombs were found by ancient treasure hunters long ago, with one famous exception . . . the tomb of Pharaoh Tutankhamun. In 1922, twelve-year-old Hussein Abdel-Rassoul was working as a water carrier for English archaeologist Howard Carter, when he stumbled across a stone step under the sand. It was the top of a staircase leading down to the sealed entrance of Tutankhamun's tomb and its treasures, undisturbed for 3,000 years.

THE MISSING KING... AND QUEEN

Four words spring from the note and it dawns on you, 'It's **THE VALLEY OF THE KINGS!**' The museum is sending a van of archaeologists there for a dig and they've offered you a ride.

Time to move!

At first glance, the Valley of the Kings in **Luxor**, Egypt, is underwhelming. A barren, sun-baked gorge with no pyramids. Yet these hills hide wonderful things . . .

You squeeze inside Tut's tomb — it's small and crowded with archaeologists. Radar images possibly show sealed doors and a corridor behind the walls. Archaeologists think it could be the missing burial chamber of Queen Nefertiti — Tutankhamun's stepmother.

But so far, they haven't found a way in. The Ghost Captain will be frustrated to miss out on stealing treasure.

Normally he leaves a clue, but with so many people inside the tomb, surely someone would have seen it by now.

Unless of course, it's . . . invisible!

You whip out your UV light and wave it across a wall at the back of the tomb. There in invisible ink . . .

CLUE

Discover how to turn these symbols into letters on p. 58.

TREASURED TEXTS

You can hardly believe your eyes. The Ghost Captain is **taunting** you!

CATCH ME IF YOU CAN I AM HIDING IN XIAN

Xi'an (pronounced 'shyann') was the beginning of the ancient Silk Road linking the Middle East and Europe with East Asia and your next destination – **China!** This 6,400-kilometre network of roads stretched across deserts and mountains and was used by merchants to trade goods.

You've arranged a lift to Cairo and will travel by Jeep from there. In the backseat, Zuri carefully opens her notebook revealing neatly drawn sketches. It holds everything you've ever needed to know about **epigraphy** – the study of ancient inscriptions.

Not just a jar ... a scroll
In 1947, two teenagers were minding their own business herding goats when they stumbled across a cave in Qumran, near Israel. They found clay jars with scrolls inside. Known as the Dead Sea Scrolls, they're some of the oldest parts of the Hebrew Bible, sometimes also known as the Old Testament. WOW!

The awesome power of the Ark
The religions of Judaism and Christianity say that God issued Ten Commandments (laws humans should live by). Engraved on to stones, they were placed inside an AWESOME golden chest called the Ark of the Covenant, then hidden in Saint Mary of Zion Cathedral in Aksum, Ethiopia. Believed to hold powers that could destroy cities, the only person to have ever seen the ark is the monk who guards it.

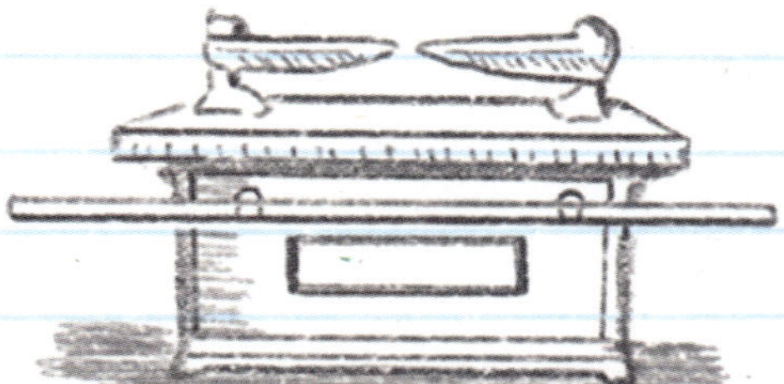

Not just a rock... a key

This broken lump of granite was dug up near the city of Rosetta, Egypt, in 1799. Back in 196 BCE temple priests wrote an unexciting message on it. Now, what IS exciting is that it was written three times in three different languages. There's ancient Greek, hieroglyphics from around 3100 BCE and Egyptian demotic, used from around 600 BCE. Scholars already knew how to read Greek, so they were able to use it to decipher hieroglyphics. BOOM! A rock became a key to the past!

Your journey along the Silk Road finally ends in Xi'an. Once the capital of China, Xi'an is now famous for something quite unexpected...

TOMB RAIDER IN XI'AN

You are soon standing at the very same spot where, in 1974, a Chinese farmer stumbled across the greatest archaeological find of the century — an 8,000-strong *terracotta army!*

'These life-size warriors have been standing guard here for over 2,000 years! Let me show you,' Zuri says, opening her trusty history book.

HISTORY OF THE WORLD

QIN SHI HUANG

In 246 BCE China's first emperor, Qin (pronounced 'chin') took the throne at age thirteen. He immediately ordered over 700,000 workers to begin building a city-sized mausoleum in preparation for his death. It's believed this underground kingdom had a ceiling that mimicked the night sky, studded with pearls that twinkled like stars.

Just like the Egyptian pharaohs, Qin would have been surrounded by his treasures for the afterlife, and so he ordered workers to begin constructing the terracotta guards. But things didn't go to plan. Qin unexpectedly died in 210 BCE, and his tomb was apparently sealed shut with the workers trapped inside - buried alive to protect the secret of the terracotta army.

'Qin is still there,' Zuri reads, 'entombed under the hill, possibly protected by an underground moat of poisonous mercury!' And nobody has dared go inside, for fear of damaging the priceless artefacts. And that's when you see...

the hole.

The Ghost Captain has tried to dig into Qin's tomb to get his hands on the treasure. By the time you reach the burial mound there are police everywhere — but it's clear the pesky pirate has already fled the scene.

In all the commotion a *piece of paper* has been trodden into the ground.

+3
PB QHAW PRYH LV WR D JROGHQ
WHPSOH LQ NHUDOD

You remember seeing something like this in your cryptology handbook. You're going to need a **cipher**.

CLUE
1
Puzzled? Go to p. 59 for some tips...

33

HISTORY OF KERALA

For many centuries, the Sree Padmanabhaswamy temple and its treasures, stored within six vaults, have been looked after by one ruling family. Five of those vaults have been opened, revealing 3,000 tonnes of gold, coins, jewellery, diamonds and artefacts. But legend has it one vault was left untouched. Known as Vault B, it is said to lie behind two chambers and a heavy steel door. The door is embossed with two enormous serpents and a vampire. They signal DANGER lies within.

One man claims the vault HAS actually been opened several times with no ill effects, but there are also stories that tell of robbers being chased away by snakes when they attempted to open it!

TREASURE IN THE TEMPLE

As you move each letter, a sentence appears:

MY NEXT MOVE IS TO A GOLDEN TEMPLE IN KERALA.

That's in India, and the drive will take about a week! Saksham types 'golden temple, Kerala' into his tablet's search engine, and the screen glows gold with images of Sree Padmanabhaswamy temple (pronounced Pad-man-ab-has-wamy).

'Good luck stealing a whole temple!' Saksham laughs. You giggle too, but as you read on you realise it's what's inside the temple that the Ghost Captain must be after.

It's night by the time your taxi pulls up outside the temple. As you run towards the front steps, you're horrified to discover snakes slithering towards you!

The Ghost Captain has tried to open Vault B, but the doors can only be opened by a holy person who is able to chant the sacred Garuda mantra to ward off evil spirits. Fortunately, the serpents have done their job and protected the treasure inside.

You scan the crowd and spot what might be a clue. Look at the front of that tuk-tuk!

2.97554S
104.77550E

CLUE

Turn to p. 59 to find out what this clue means.

THE LOST CITIES

2.97554S
104.77550E

'I know what they are!' Saksham says. 'They're GPS coordinates.'
He takes out his tablet and types the numbers into his map app.
They lead to . . . **Palembang** in Indonesia.

You jump in the tuk-tuk and head to the port to stow away on a ship to Indonesia. Hiding among the crates in the cargo hold, Saksham shares his travel magazine to pass the time.

Kerala

Palembang

ON THE TRAIL
LOST CITIES

Over centuries, civilisations have crumbled – lost to war, disease or natural disasters. Finding them offers the greatest treasures of all . . . clues to our past.

Eaten by the forest
Cambodia's Buddhist temple complex, Angkor Wat, was swallowed by the jungle many centuries ago, before being revealed to the outside world in the 1800s, covered in a tangle of vines.

Sleeping beneath the ash
When Italy's Mount Vesuvius erupted in 79 CE, the ancient Roman city of Pompeii was destroyed. In the late sixteenth century, it was found, preserved under a deep layer of volcanic ash.

The lost city of gold
In the sixteenth century, Spanish explorers heard of a chieftain living high in the Andes Mountains, who would cover himself in gold dust and wade into a lake. They believed the chieftain built a kingdom of gold – perhaps it was the city 'Eldorado', a word they'd heard used by local indigenous people. So began centuries of bloody conquests in South America. While the Spanish did find gold, they never found a city made of gold. Historians now believe Eldorado wasn't a place, it was a man – the chieftain of the Muisca people. Eldorado means 'the golden one'.

THE ISLAND OF GOLD

The ship finally docks in **Palembang**, and you're spotted by the crew — oops! You escape by leaping on to a passing boat heading up the Musi River.

Your boat weaves past people going about their lives, doing the washing, fishing and mending nets.

As you round the bend, Saksham spots **divers** hauling up objects from the riverbed. The dock is covered in treasure: temple bells, coins and even a life-sized statue of Buddha.

'Hey, what's all this?' Zuri asks.

A diver takes off his mask and explains they've found the treasure from the long-lost *Island of Gold*.

HISTORY OF THE WORLD
THE FLOATING KINGDOM

From the seventh to the thirteenth century, Palembang was home to the Srivijaya (pronounced Sriv-ee-jie-ah) empire. This floating kingdom was both wealthy and powerful, controlling important parts of the maritime Silk Road. Its people were boat people, who lived in floating bamboo houses on the river. Srivijaya ruled Indonesia for just over 600 years, until it sank without a trace. Did a volcanic eruption or a flood cause Srivijaya to disappear? Was the empire overcome by a rival kingdom? Or did the people of Srivijaya throw their treasures into the river as an offering to the gods?

As you stare, gobsmacked by the treasure haul, a diver taps you on the shoulder. 'I'm supposed to give you this,' she shrugs.

It's a soggy map covered in *letters* and *lines.*

'It's got instructions on the other side,' Saksham says. 'Maybe if we follow them, it'll lead us across the map?'

It says: 'I'm **flying** to Seattle, then I'll take a **bus**. From there, I will catch a **train** and next travel by **car**. Where do I end up?'

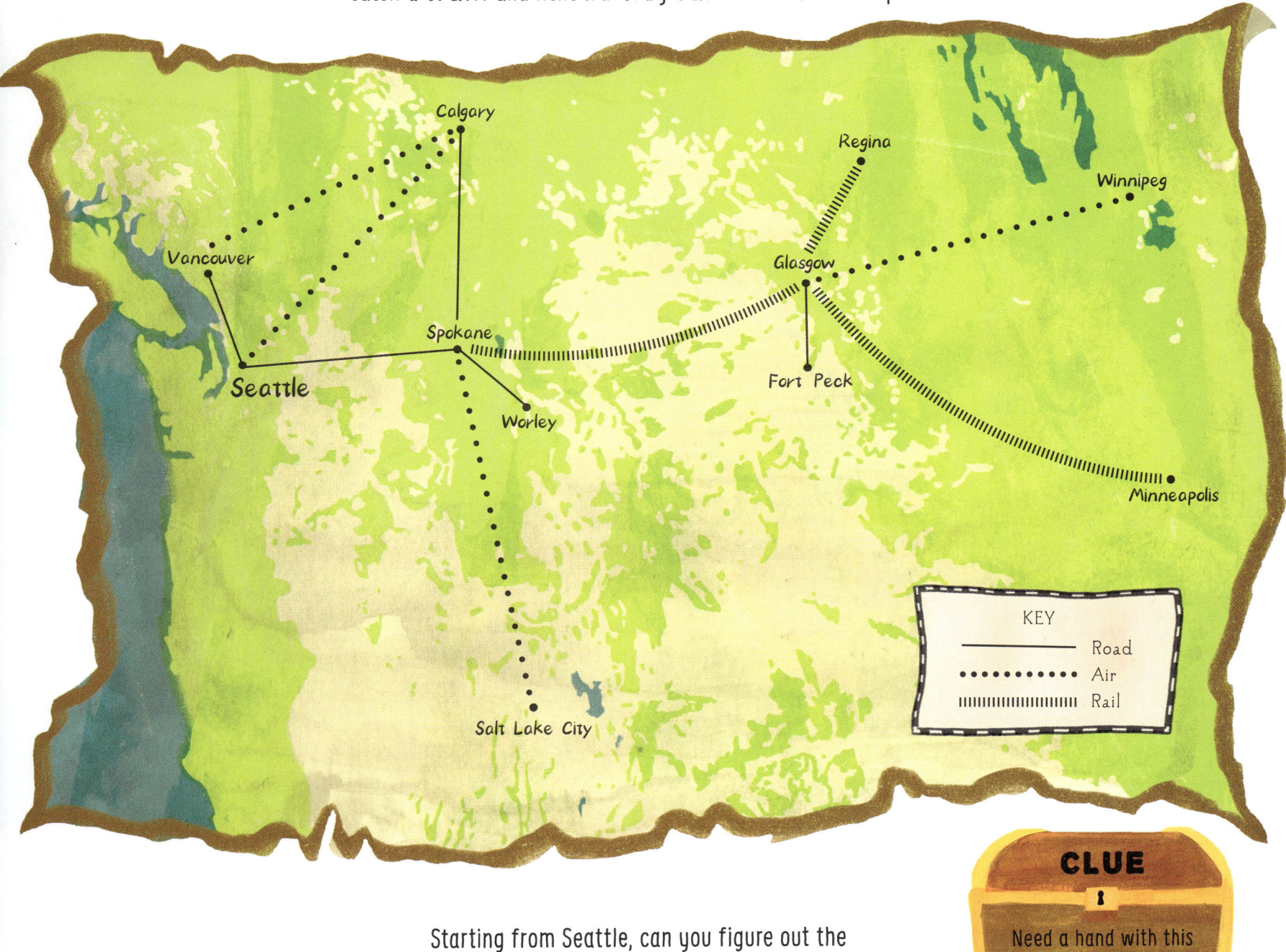

KEY
— Road
• • • • Air
||||||||| Rail

Starting from Seattle, can you figure out the Ghost Captain's route to his next destination?

CLUE

Need a hand with this puzzle? Turn to p. 60.

39

HISTORY OF THE HELL CREEK FORMATION

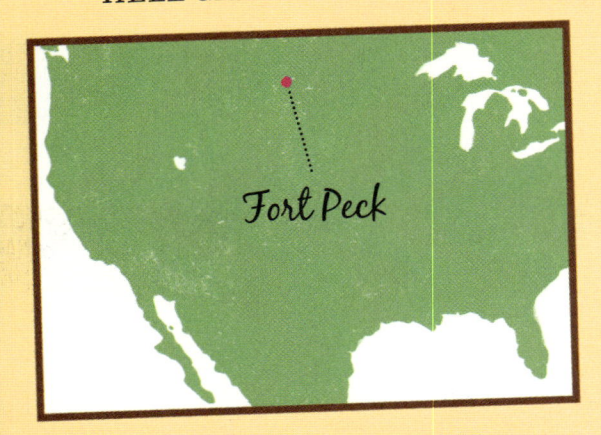

Fort Peck

On the dry and rocky lands of Montana, North Dakota, South Dakota and Wyoming in the USA, hoodoos – mushroom-shaped rocks – dot the landscape. This is the Hell Creek Formation, where the rocks have been eroded just enough to reveal a very special kind of treasure – dinosaur fossils, many from the late Cretaceous period, some 67 million years ago.

Discovering dinosaur bones is exciting because the chance of a creature being fossilised in the first place is slim; it must be buried fast so that it doesn't decompose or get eaten by something else. That's why unearthing big fossils has become BIG business, with wealthy collectors paying millions of pounds for them.

A BONE TO PICK WITH YOU

After carefully tracing the Ghost Captain's route across the map, your finger ends on . . .

Fort Peck!

Saksham checks his map. 'Fort Peck is part of the *Hell Creek formation*,' Saksham says, 'and that's dinosaur country!'

Your car finally rolls into Fort Peck, where a group of people are staring at the ground. 'It's a Tyrannosaurus rex!' Saksham yells, and in no time, he's rattling off his best fossil facts.

Saksham says scientists believe only 20,000 T. rexes ever roamed the planet at any one time. That's why fewer than a hundred T. rex skeletons have ever been found, and for most of them, only a single bone.

'That makes this fossil especially precious,' a palaeontologist adds. 'This skeleton is almost complete and includes the first T. rex forearm ever found.'

Suddenly there's a shout on the other side of the dig. A T. rex tooth is missing and nobody can see a thing because the culprit has just taken off in a helicopter, whipping up a cloud of dust. The Ghost Captain strikes again.

As the dust clears, you discover the tooth has been hammered into a hoodoo, pinning a message in place. It's another clue!

T _ E / M _ M M _ T _ /
15 1 6 4 11 4 4 10 15 1

G _ _ V E y _ _ D / I _ /
14 2 11 12 6 7 11 2 8   9 13

M E _ I _ _ / _ I T y
4 6 5 9 3 10   3 9 15 7

A	C	D	E	G	H	I	M	N	O	R	T	V	X	Y
		8	6	14		9	4				15	12		7

CLUE

For help decrypting the cryptogram go to p. 60.

FAMOUS FOSSILS

Wow, that puzzle was especially tricky, but you still solved it: **The Mammoth Graveyard** in **Mexico City!** And in a stroke of luck the team have offered you a ride. Under the van's backseat, you find a box of dusty sketchbooks with drawings of world-famous fossils.

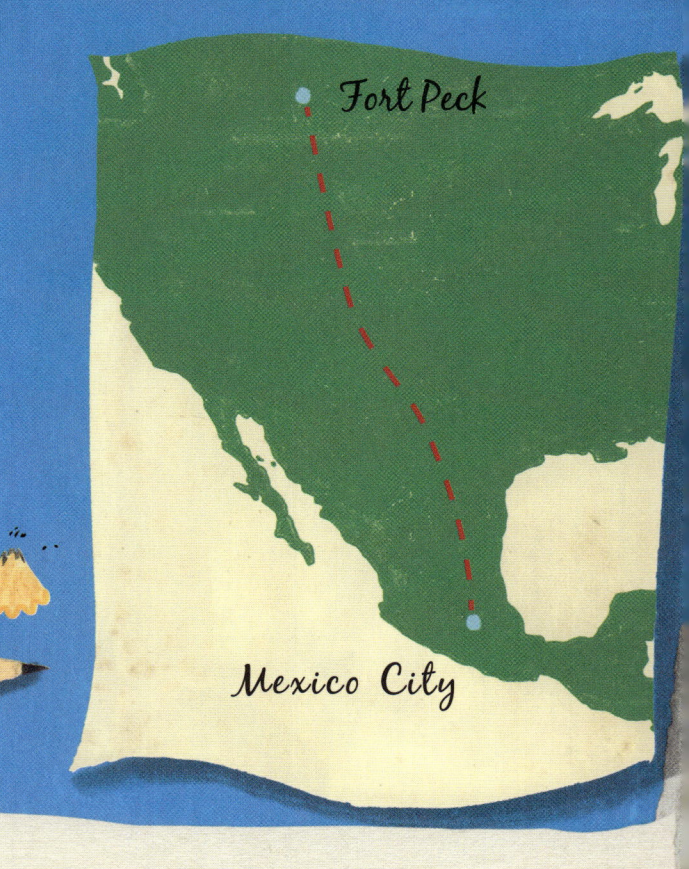

Fort Peck

Mexico City

Here lies the car-park King

The Lost King

In 1483, King Edward IV of England died. His brother Richard III was named 'protector of the realm' until one of Edward's two young sons were old enough to take the throne. Desperate to have the throne for himself, Richard locked the young princes in the Tower of London, and they were never seen again. Richard III became king, but his reign was short-lived. He died in battle in 1485 and was buried at Grey Friars Church in Leicester, England.

A few decades later, King Henry VIII was angry at the church for not allowing him to divorce his first wife. He made himself head of the church and demolished many religious buildings, including Grey Friars. Richard III's grave was lost – but not forgotten. Using old maps, archaeologists traced its location to under a car park in Leicester!

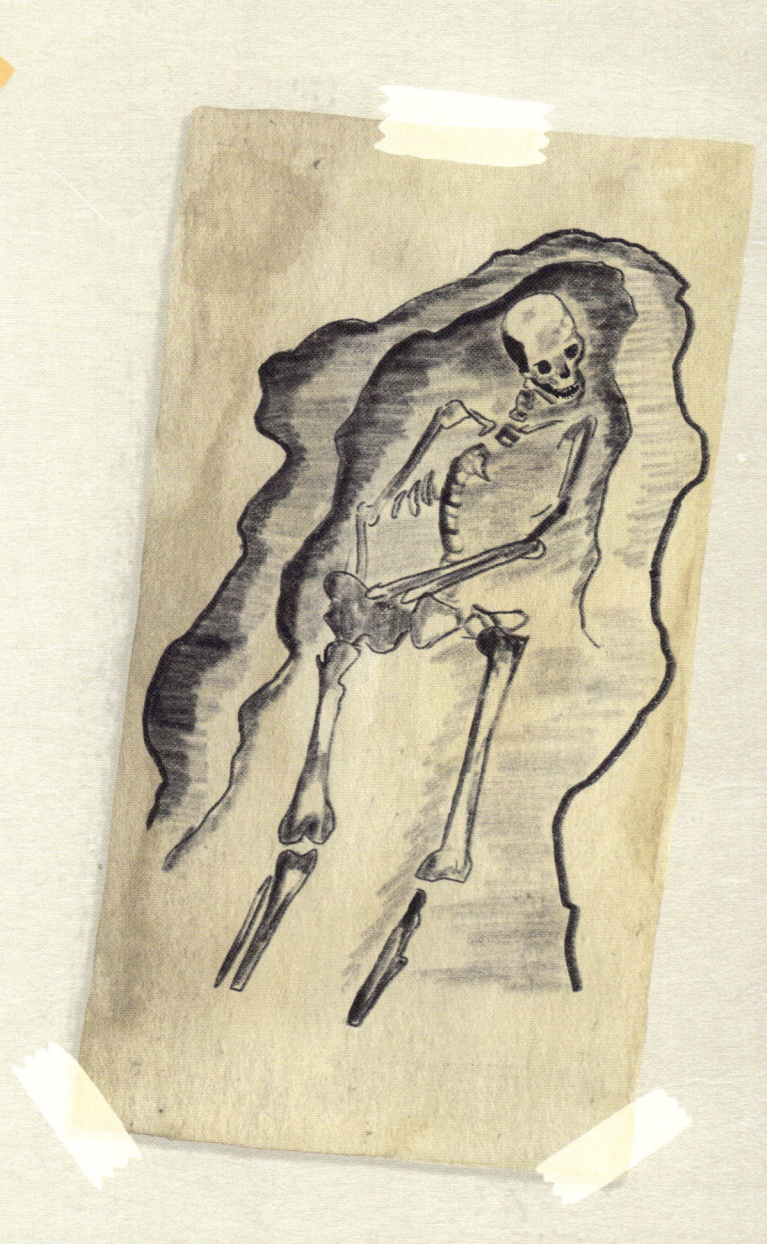

Giant 'lizard' discovered in Oxfordshire, UK

In 1824, geologist William Buckland unwittingly came up with the first scientific description of a dinosaur! What he thought was a giant lizard was in fact a Megalosaurus, a fierce predator with blade-like teeth.

The case of the disappearing bones

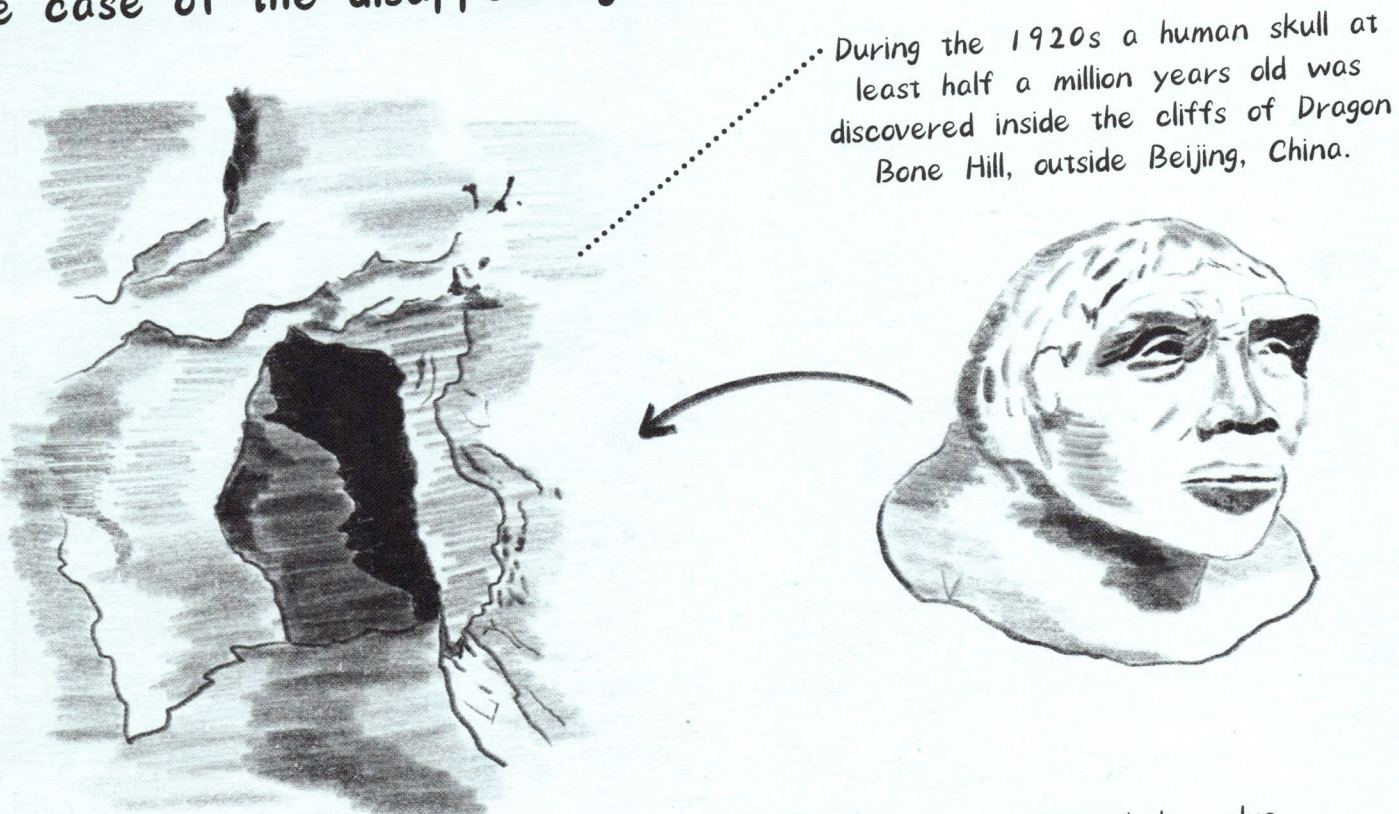

During the 1920s a human skull at least half a million years old was discovered inside the cliffs of Dragon Bone Hill, outside Beijing, China.

Named Peking Man, he was identified as a homo erectus and provided a clue to how modern humans evolved. The fossils found in the area proved that Peking Man handled fire, made clothes and used tools. During the Second World War, the fossils were packed up to send to the USA, but they were never seen again. Did they make it onto a ship only to be sunk in the war? Or are they buried under a car park too?

STUCK IN THE MUD

After two days' drive, squished into a van with too many palaeontologists, a construction site comes into view. You're outside **Mexico City** where work is under way on a new airport. Except every time the crews dig into the ground ... they find mammoth bones.

HISTORY OF THE WORLD
MAMMOTH MAMMOTHS

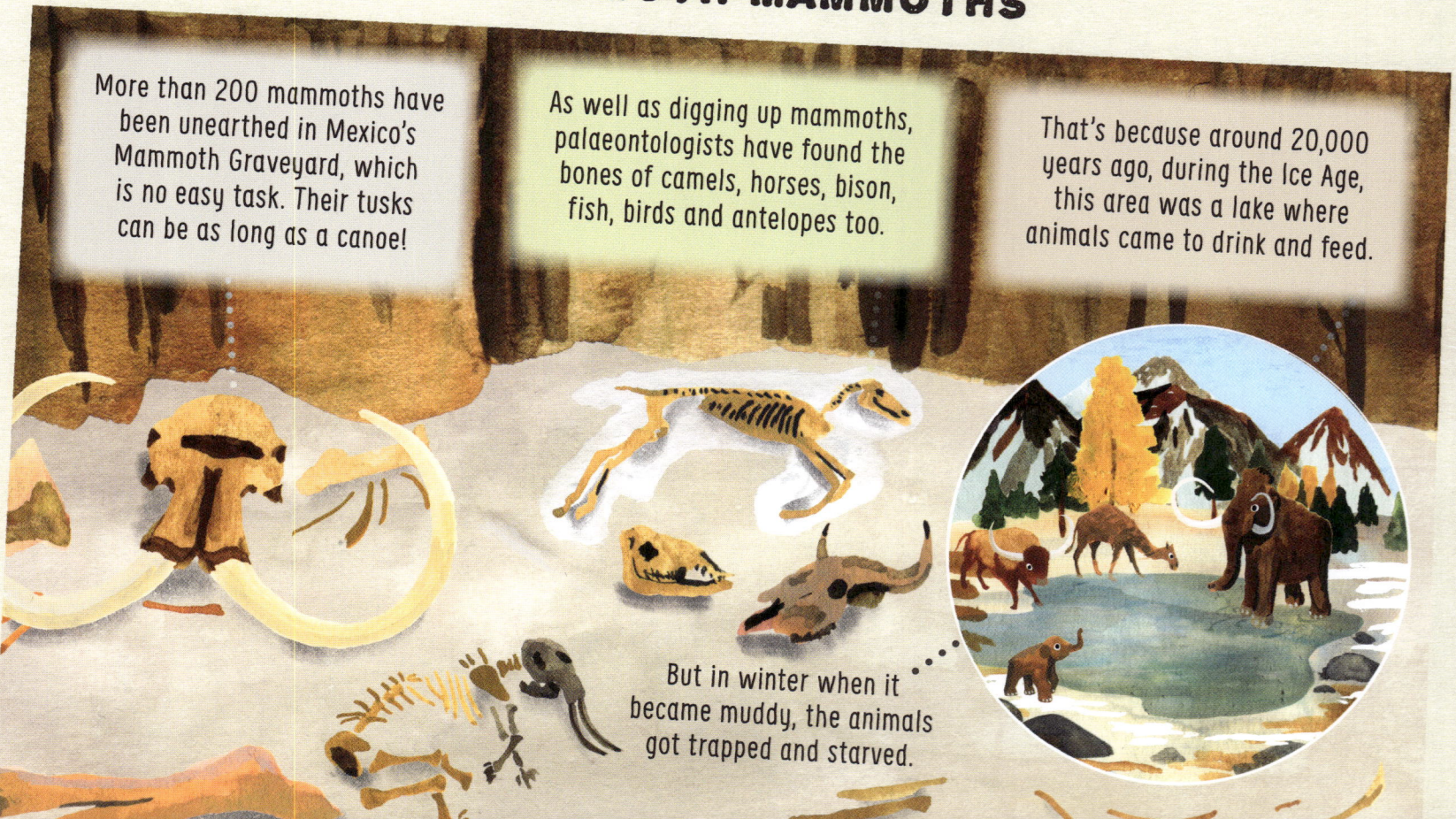

More than 200 mammoths have been unearthed in Mexico's Mammoth Graveyard, which is no easy task. Their tusks can be as long as a canoe!

As well as digging up mammoths, palaeontologists have found the bones of camels, horses, bison, fish, birds and antelopes too.

That's because around 20,000 years ago, during the Ice Age, this area was a lake where animals came to drink and feed.

But in winter when it became muddy, the animals got trapped and starved.

44

This is not just a rare glimpse into the past; a mammoth tusk can fetch a hefty price at auction. Clearly this is what the Ghost Captain has in mind, as you catch him red-handed, struggling to drag a heavy tusk over the bank.

'Hands off that tusk!' you shout.

Dropping the tusk, the Ghost Captain makes a run for it. You're no slowpoke though, and quickly gain ground. You stretch out your hand and grab a fistful of his cloak.

'Ha! Got you now!' you cry.

The Ghost Captain shakes off his cloak, and it billows in the wind, tangling around your face. You claw it off, but he's vanished. You really thought you had him this time, but now all you've got is his moth-eaten cloak.

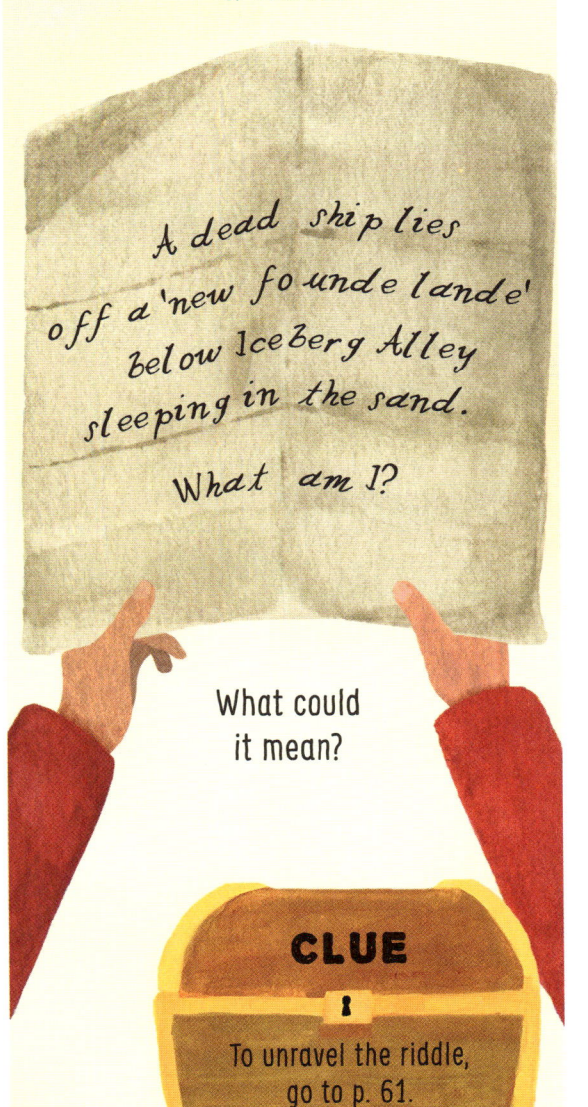

But wait . . . a pocket. And inside the pocket . . . *a note.*

A dead ship lies off a 'new founde lande' below Iceberg Alley sleeping in the sand.

What am I?

What could it mean?

CLUE

To unravel the riddle, go to p. 61.

✳ HISTORY OF THE TITANIC ✳

Saint John's (Newfoundland)

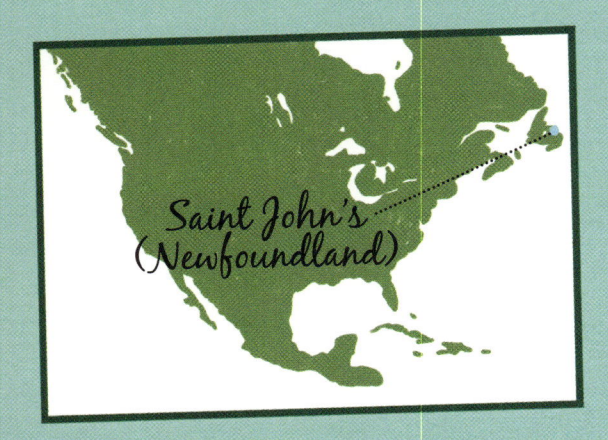

The *Titanic* has lain about 4,000 metres down on the floor of the Atlantic Ocean for over a hundred years. It's rusted and covered in bacteria that's slowly eating through its iron hull. Scientists predict in 20 years the wreckage will be gone. But what of the treasures onboard?

When the *Titanic* sank, it took its wealthy passengers' belongings with it. While some have been retrieved, many are still down there, from precious jewels and grand pianos, to artwork, a jewel-encrusted book and even a car!

TREASURES OF THE TITANIC

'I know this one!' Zuri says triumphantly. 'Dead Ship could be code for sunken ship. And those words look like old English for **Newfoundland** in *Canada*. And we all know what hit an iceberg off Canada, right? The *TITANIC*! I bet the Ghost Captain's after its sunken treasures!'

After endless bus rides, taxis and a ferry, you arrive in Saint John's, where an expedition team are heading out to the wreck of the *Titanic*. You convince them to let you onboard, and when the boat arrives at the wreck site, you squeeze inside the mini submarine and *DIVE!*

The sub's bright lights cut through the gloom as you glide over the wreckage. The *Titanic* split in two as it sunk. The bow is mostly intact; you can make out every steel rivet and porthole. And, as your spotlight sweeps across the deck, Saksham shouts: 'Look, a flag!'

A flag is flying in the current. Except it's not just any flag. As you zoom in on the cameras you see that the Ghost Captain has beaten you down to the wreck and has hoisted up another **puzzle!**

CLUES
1. A sunken sea vessel on the ocean floor is said to be...?
2. A European language spoken in 20 countries.
3. A type of sailing ship used from the fifteenth to eighteenth centuries.
4. The opposite of far.
5. A country found in South America, bordering the Caribbean Sea and the South Pacific Ocean.

1. S _ _ _ _ _ _ _ _ (C A T across top)
2. S _ _ _ _ _ (T)
3. _ _ _ _ _ _ (G)
4. _ _ _ _ (E N)
5. C _ _ _ _ _ _ _

CLUE

For some handy hints, turn to p. 61.

47

RICHES IN THE WRECKS

The answers to the crossword —

SHIPWRECKED SPANISH GALLEON NEAR COLOMBIA

— reveals another word running down the puzzle. It's the Ghost Captain's next destination.

'Easy,' Saksham smiles, waving his map in the air. 'It's **Cartagena** in Colombia.' (Pronounced kaa-tuh-heh-nuh.)

Zuri gets to work researching famous shipwrecks as your boat sets sail for Colombia.

BLACKBEARD'S BOOTY!

In the 1700s the notorious pirate Blackbeard terrorised the seas aboard the *Queen Anne's Revenge*. With 40 cannons the ship was believed near-unsinkable, until . . . she sunk! In 1718, the *Queen Anne's Revenge* ran aground on a sandbar off the coast of North Carolina, USA, forcing Blackbeard to take his treasure and abandon ship. He died a few months later battling the British, and if the stories are true, they turned his skull into a punchbowl! As for the *Queen Anne's Revenge*, she wasn't seen again until treasure hunters discovered her in 1996. They found Blackbeard's cannons and his cutlass onboard . . . but they never found his gold.

CASE UNSOLVED

TREASURE HUNTERS HIT THE JACKPOT...

...when they discovered the remains of the Spanish warship *Nuestra Señora de las Mercedes* (*Our Lady of Mercedes*) sunk by the British navy in 1804. She went to a watery grave in the Atlantic Ocean off Portugal, still clutching around 600,000 gold and silver coins. They're now on display in Spain.

CASE SOLVED ✓

THE GHOST SHIP ENDURES

In 1915, polar explorer Sir Ernest Shackleton was attempting the first land crossing of Antarctica when his ship, *Endurance*, was crushed by moving pack ice (floating sea ice). Forced to abandon ship, Shackleton helplessly watched on as *Endurance* sank into the Weddell Sea. *Endurance* wasn't seen again until 2022 when scientists discovered her sat proudly upright on the seabed. She looked exactly as she did the day she sank, her name clearly visible on the stern.

CASE SOLVED ✓

Saint John's (Newfoundland)

Cartagena

49

THE SINKING OF THE SAN JOSÉ

The Caribbean may feel like paradise, but in the seventeenth century, paradise was full of pirates.

Pirates hid among the Caribbean's islands and bays, waiting for Spanish galleons loaded with treasure to sail by. The pirates would hoist up the Jolly Roger flag, and with the skull and crossbones flying, they'd attack.

If dodging pirates wasn't bad enough, crews also had to navigate wild weather and coral reefs that could tear open their hull. It's thought that around 600 ships have sunk in this part of the world, but the holy grail of shipwrecks is the long-lost *San José*.

THE HOLY GRAIL OF SHIPWRECKS

1708 'Clear the decks!' 'Fire at will!'

The British and the Spanish are at it again, this time off the coast of Cartagena in Colombia.

It's a disaster for the Spanish, as their ship the *San José* . . .

. . . bursts into flames and sinks, dragging down 600 men . . .

. . . and BILLIONS of pounds in Maya gold, silver and jewels.

For more than 300 years she lay hidden off the coast of Cartagena, until . . .

. . . TA DA! Scientists find her.

She's mine!

Hands off! She belongs to us.

Back off! We found her first!

And the *San José*'s toughest battle began . . . authorities are still fighting over who owns her today.

You'd bet a bunch of bullion that the Ghost Captain is after the treasures of the *San José*!

You arrive in Cartagena and head for the tourist information kiosk to find out if there's any way to see the sunken galleon. But on the way something catches Zuri's eye. Pinned to a palm tree is . . .

...A TREASURE MAP!

The map shows a dotted line leaving Cartagena and ending at a huge X marking a spot over **Île Sainte-Marie**, a small island off Madagascar in the Indian Ocean.

The Ghost Captain is summoning you across the ocean. This must be the end of the journey; you can feel it in your bones. Tighten your life jackets, it's going be a rough ride!

You finally drop anchor in the harbour of Ambodifotatra, and collapse in a soggy heap. Is it possible that by gaining your sea legs, you've lost your land legs? That was hands-down the worst journey of the whole expedition. But my goodness, did the Ghost Captain save the best for last — this is paradise ... for pirates.

HISTORY OF THE WORLD

Historians think that in the seventeenth and eighteenth centuries more than 1,000 pirates came ashore on Île Sainte-Marie to hide, after plundering ships in the Caribbean. It's believed 13 shipwrecks are hidden in these waters, including Captain Kidd's *Adventure Galley*. Treasure hunters suspect Kidd may have sunk his treasure in the surrounding sea.

The 'X' on the map leads you to a hill just across the bay.
You hike up a lone track, walk the plank across a mangrove creek and discover . . .

the crumbling remains of a pirates' graveyard.

Among the long grass and swaying palm are headstones — one is etched with a skull and crossbones!

And that's when you see . . .

53

...THE GHOST CAPTAIN.

As he slowly turns towards you,
your mouth drops open in surprise.
The Ghost Captain is... *a woman!*

'I'm Magnolia Kidd. What took you so long?'

Magnolia Kidd is NOT a ghost, she's Captain Kidd's rascal of a great-granddaughter — nine times removed. And she's led you on an astonishing adventure to challenge your treasure-hunting skills. At every step she's left a breadcrumb-trail of clues for you to follow.

'It was all a test, and you passed with flying colours,' Magnolia says with a laugh. It turns out you're everything Magnolia could have hoped for from a first mate.

☑ 1. You can read maps
☑ 2. Crack codes
☑ 3. Unravel riddles
☑ 4. Your sea legs aren't bad either.

As for Captain Kidd's lost treasure . . . 'I don't know where it is,' Magnolia sighs, 'but what I *do* know is that I've now met the right people to help me find it. So, what do you say?'

As the sun dips into the sea, setting the sky alight you all hurriedly clamber aboard Magnolia's ship, the *Broken Rope*. The wind catches in the sails, sweeping you forward on another adventure to discover if X really does *mark the spot*!

CAN I GIVE YOU A CLUE?

Page 11: Puzzled by a pigpen cipher?

Some of the earliest examples of a pigpen cipher were used by a secret society known as the Freemasons in the eighteenth century. To crack the code, match the symbols on the visitor book with the letters in the grid below. For instance ⌐ is L, the □ is E and < is U. P.S. Could this message be written in French?

Key:

A	B	C
D	E	F
G	H	I

Page 15: Making sense of maps

55N 37E are map coordinates! You can pinpoint any place on Earth using a series of numbers called coordinates. We get these numbers by dividing Earth into a grid. The lines running across (horizontally) are called latitude lines. The lines running down (vertically) are called longitude lines.

The equator wraps around the centre of Earth at 0 degrees latitude. Each latitude line north or south of the equator increases by 1 degree to 90 degrees.

The vertical lines of longitude are called Meridian lines. They begin at 0 degrees longitude in Greenwich, London. Each longitude line east or west of Greenwich increases by 1 degree to 180 degrees.

You've been given the coordinates 55°N (latitude) and 37°E (longitude). Turn to the map on pages 62–63. Put your left finger roughly on 55°N and your right finger on 37°E. Follow the lines and roughly where your fingers meet is the next location.

Page 17: Try using a mirror!

Page 21: Muddled by Morse code?

All these dots and dashes represent different letters. Created by Samuel F. B. Morse in the 1830s, Morse code allowed messages to be sent by telegraph in minutes, rather than waiting weeks for a letter to arrive in the post. The signals travelled down wires strung up above towns, using pulses of electricity to signal to a machine that would make marks on a piece of paper. Match the dots and dashes to the key below to decipher the message. Once you have deciphered the code, you may want to check the map on pages 62–63.

.... . .-. -.. ..-. --- .-. -..

-- --- ..- -. - .- .. -. ...

.--. .. -.- ...

Key:

A	.-	N	-.
B	-...	O	---
C	-.-.	P	.--.
D	-..	Q	--.-
E	.	R	.-.
F	..-.	S	...
G	--.	T	-
H	....	U	..-
I	..	V	...-
J	.---	W	.--
K	-.-	X	-..-
L	.-..	Y	-.--
M	--	Z	--..

Page 23: Don't let runes ruin your day

The Nordic Vikings had their own alphabet called runes, where symbols were used to represent sounds. There are only 16 symbols, compared to the 26 letters in our alphabet, so the spelling won't be the same as it is today. But if you say it out loud it will all make sense.

ᚾᚭᚱᛁᛋᚼᛅᛏ ᛘᚢᛋᛁᚢᛘ

ᛁᚠ ᛋᚴᚭᛏᛚᛅᚾᛏ

Key:

ᚠᚢᚦᛅᚱᚴ   ᚼᚾᛁᛅᛋ   ᛏᛒᛘᛚᛦ
fuþąrk   hnias   tbmlR

Page 27: Riddle me this

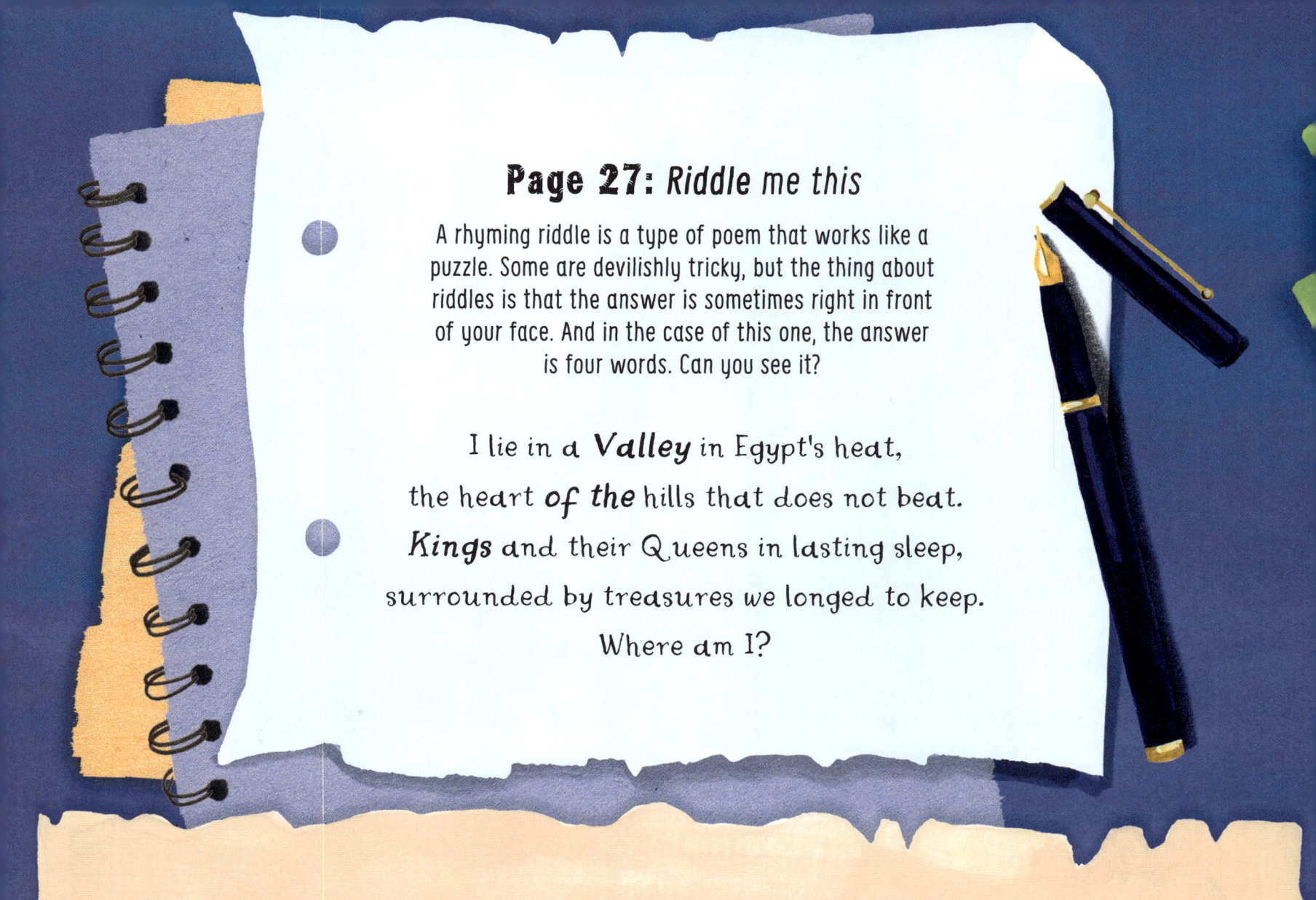

A rhyming riddle is a type of poem that works like a puzzle. Some are devilishly tricky, but the thing about riddles is that the answer is sometimes right in front of your face. And in the case of this one, the answer is four words. Can you see it?

I lie in a **Valley** in Egypt's heat,
the heart **of the** hills that does not beat.
Kings and their Queens in lasting sleep,
surrounded by treasures we longed to keep.
Where am I?

Page 29: In a huff over hieroglyphics?

Imagine how long it must have taken to write anything in ancient Egypt! These hieroglyphic symbols were mostly used by priests and to decorate the walls of temples. This alphabet has 29 symbols — three more than ours. But hieroglyphics was a very complex language. There were also signs to represent a combination of sounds, and ones with pictures of objects. Why not have a crack at using this alphabet to decipher the secret message below! You may want to check one of the words in this message against the map on pages 62-63.

HIEROGLYPHIC ALPHABET

Page 33: Hail, Caesar!

A Caesar shift cipher got its name because it was used by general Julius Caesar who ruled Rome from 46–44 BCE. He used it to encrypt secret messages, by lining up 2 rows of 26 boxes and putting a letter from the alphabet in each box. This one works by moving the top row of letters 3 places to the right, which explains the '+3' at the top of your piece of paper. Can you figure out what the message means? Hint: Use the shifted alphabet to find the true letter in the row above. For instance, 'P' is 'M' and 'B' is 'Y'.

+3

PB QHAW PRYH LV WR D JROGHQ

WHPSOH LQ NHUDOD

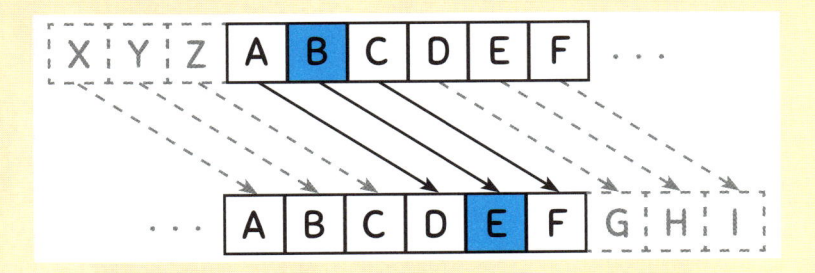

Standard alphabet

| A | B | C | D | E | F | G | H | I | J | K | L | M | N | O | P | Q | R | S | T | U | V | W | X | Y | Z |
| D | E | F | G | H | I | J | K | L | M | N | O | P | Q | R | S | T | U | V | W | X | Y | Z | A | B | C |

Shifted alphabet

Page 35: What is this number nonsense?

Obviously, this isn't a number plate. Look at it, it's enormous! In fact, it looks rather suspiciously like GPS coordinates. They start off like map coordinates, and then give you even more detail to pinpoint a precise location on the planet. And they can do that thanks to satellites orbiting Earth.

To solve this puzzle, all you need to do is type the coordinates into a search engine or an online map app, leaving a space between 2.97554S and 104.77550E. Good luck!

Page 39: I'm routing for you!

Can you trace the Ghost Captain's route? After flying to Seattle in America, he takes a bus, and we all know that buses travel by ROAD. After that he goes by train, and they whizz along RAIL tracks. Finally, he goes by car, and that means he's back on the ROAD. Where does that lead you?

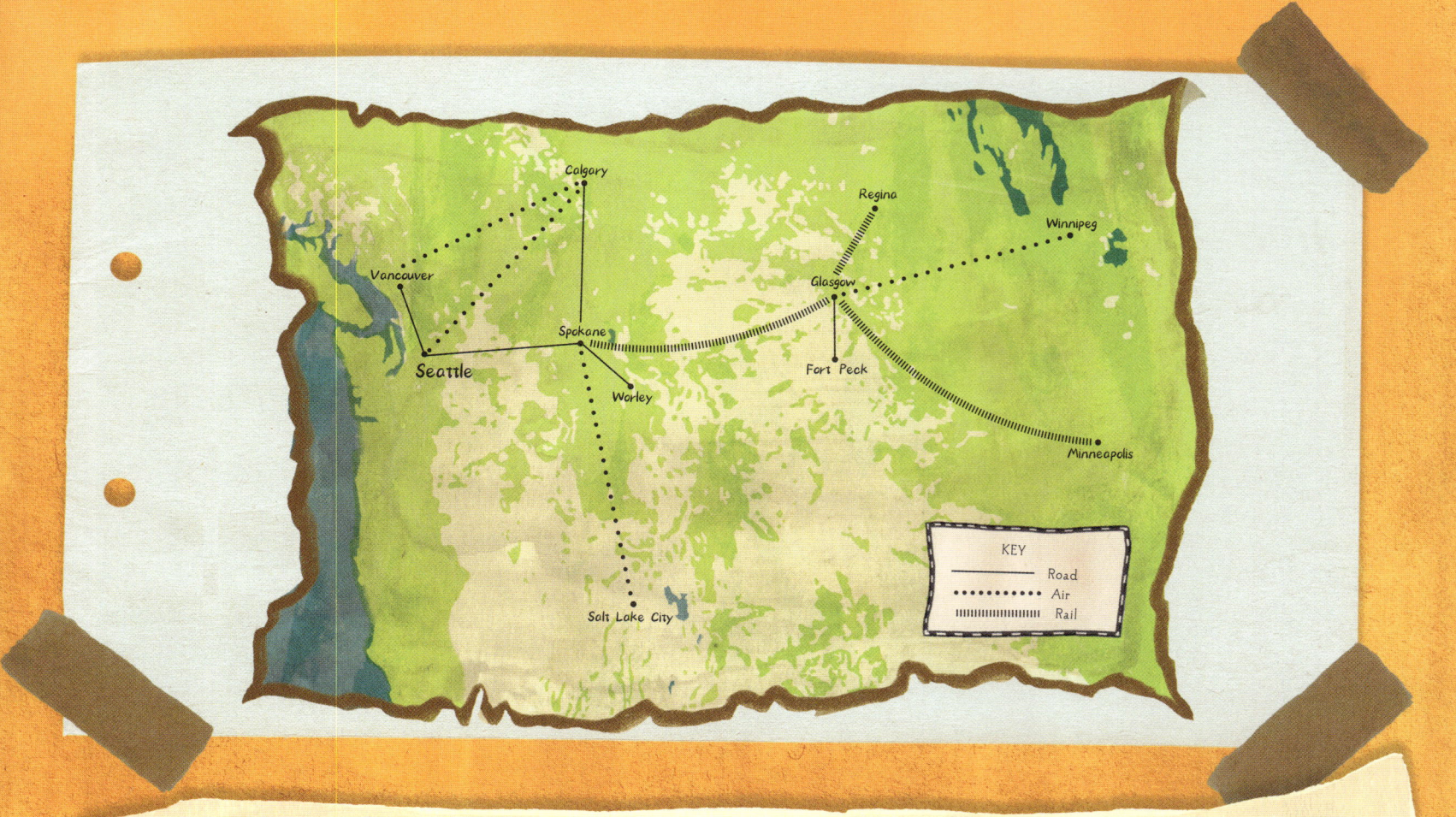

KEY
— Road
····· Air
▬▬▬ Rail

Page 41: Crack on with this cryptogram

Cryptograms were a game created by monks in the Middle Ages and later adopted by militaries to encrypt messages. To solve this type of puzzle you need to work out which number represents which letter. As young cryptologists, you've been given a head start, with a few letters already in place. The best place to start in solving a cryptogram is to . . .

1. Solve the short words first. Words that are one letter long are A or I. Common two-letter words are OF, TO, IN, IS, IT, AS, HE, BE, BY, ON, OR, AT, MY.
2. Solve the three-letter words next.
3. Look for double letters.
4. Look for diagraphs — letters that 'pair up', such as CH, SH, TH, PH, CK, QU, WH.

T _ E / M _ M M _ T _ /
15 1 6 4 11 4 4 10 15 1

G _ _ V E Y _ _ D / I _ /
14 2 11 12 6 7 11 2 8 9 13

M E _ I _ _ / _ I T Y
4 6 5 9 3 10 3 9 15 7

A	C	D	E	G	H	I	M	N	O	R	T	V	X	Y
	8	6	14		9	4					15	12		7

Page 45: Riddle me that

Try reading this line by line. What could a dead ship be? What place does 'new founde lande' sound like when you say it out aloud? Is there a place that sounds similar to those words on the map on pages 62–63? Where is Iceberg Alley? (If you get really stuck, a cheeky online search of 'Iceberg Alley' should reveal the truth.)

A dead ship lies

off a 'new founde lande'

below **Iceberg Alley**

sleeping in the sand.

What am I?

Page 47: Double trouble – double puzzle

It's a crossword with a hidden answer inside! Once you've solved the crossword clues, you'll be able to fill in the missing letters to figure out where the Ghost Captain has gone next. Check the map on pages 62–63 for this city.

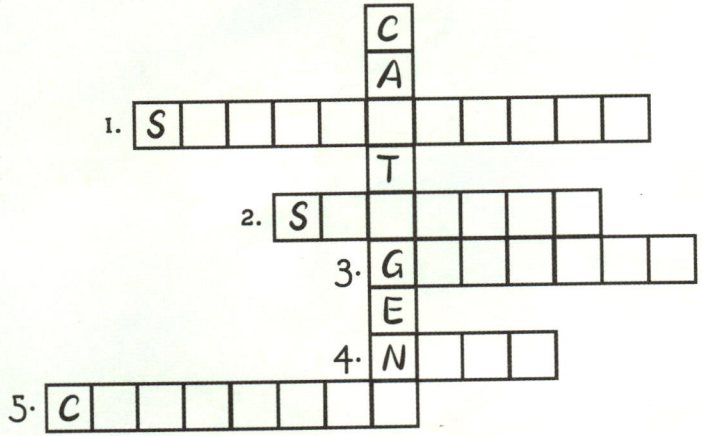

```
              C
              A
   1. S _ _ _ _ _ _ _
              T
   2.    S _ _ _ _ _ _
              G
   3.      _ _ _ _ _ _ _
              E
   4.      _ _ N _ _
   5. C _ _ _ _ _ _ _
```

CLUES

1. A sunken sea vessel on the ocean floor is said to be...?
2. A European language spoken in 20 countries.
3. A type of sailing ship used from the fifteenth to eighteenth centuries.
4. The opposite of far.
5. A country found in South America, bordering the Caribbean Sea and the South Pacific Ocean.

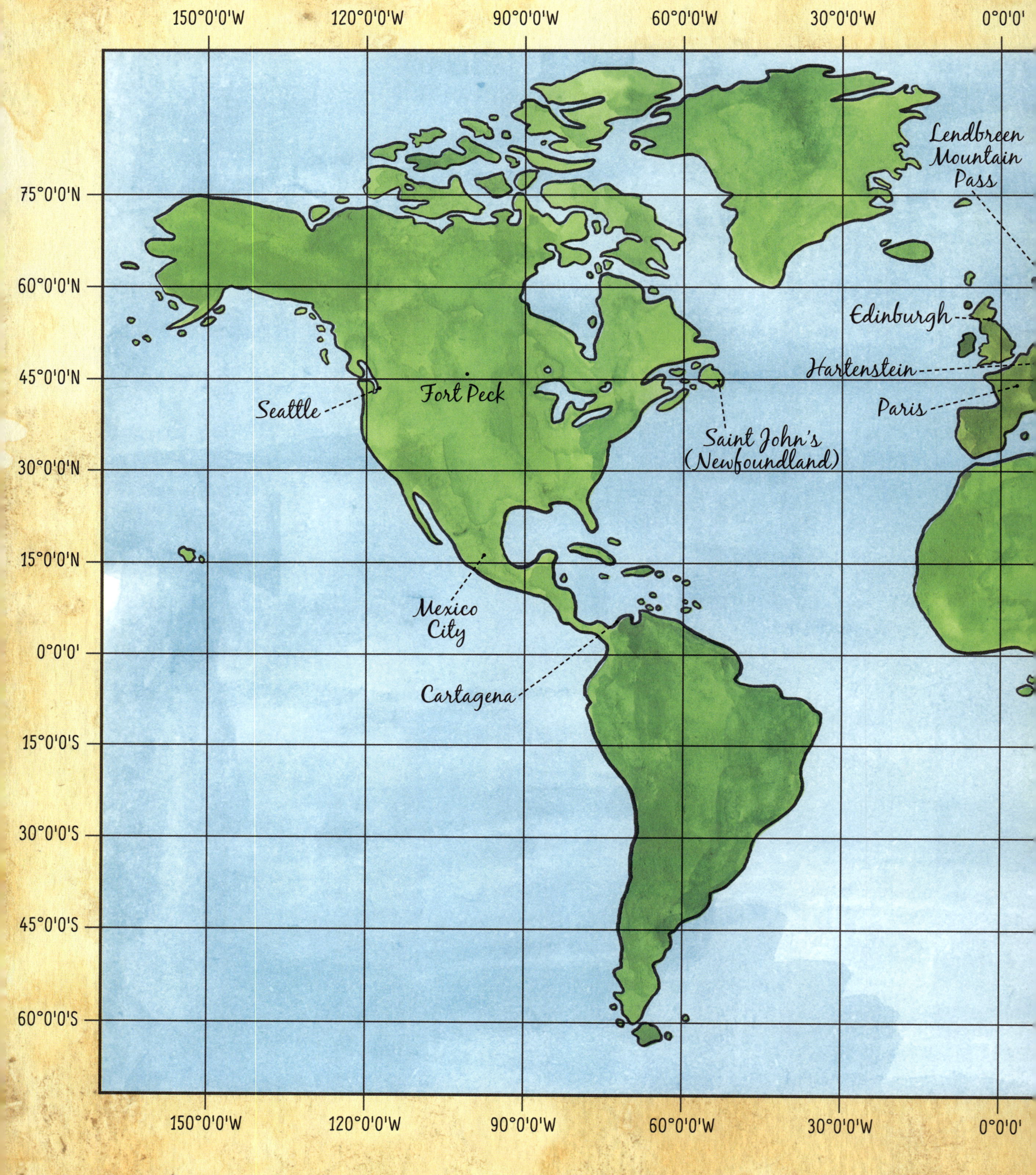
150°0'0'W
120°0'0'W
90°0'0'W
60°0'0'W
30°0'0'W
0°0'0'
75°0'0'N
60°0'0'N
45°0'0'N
30°0'0'N
15°0'0'N
0°0'0'
15°0'0'S
30°0'0'S
45°0'0'S
60°0'0'S
Lendbreen Mountain Pass
Edinburgh
Hartenstein
Paris
Seattle
Fort Peck
Saint John's (Newfoundland)
Mexico City
Cartagena

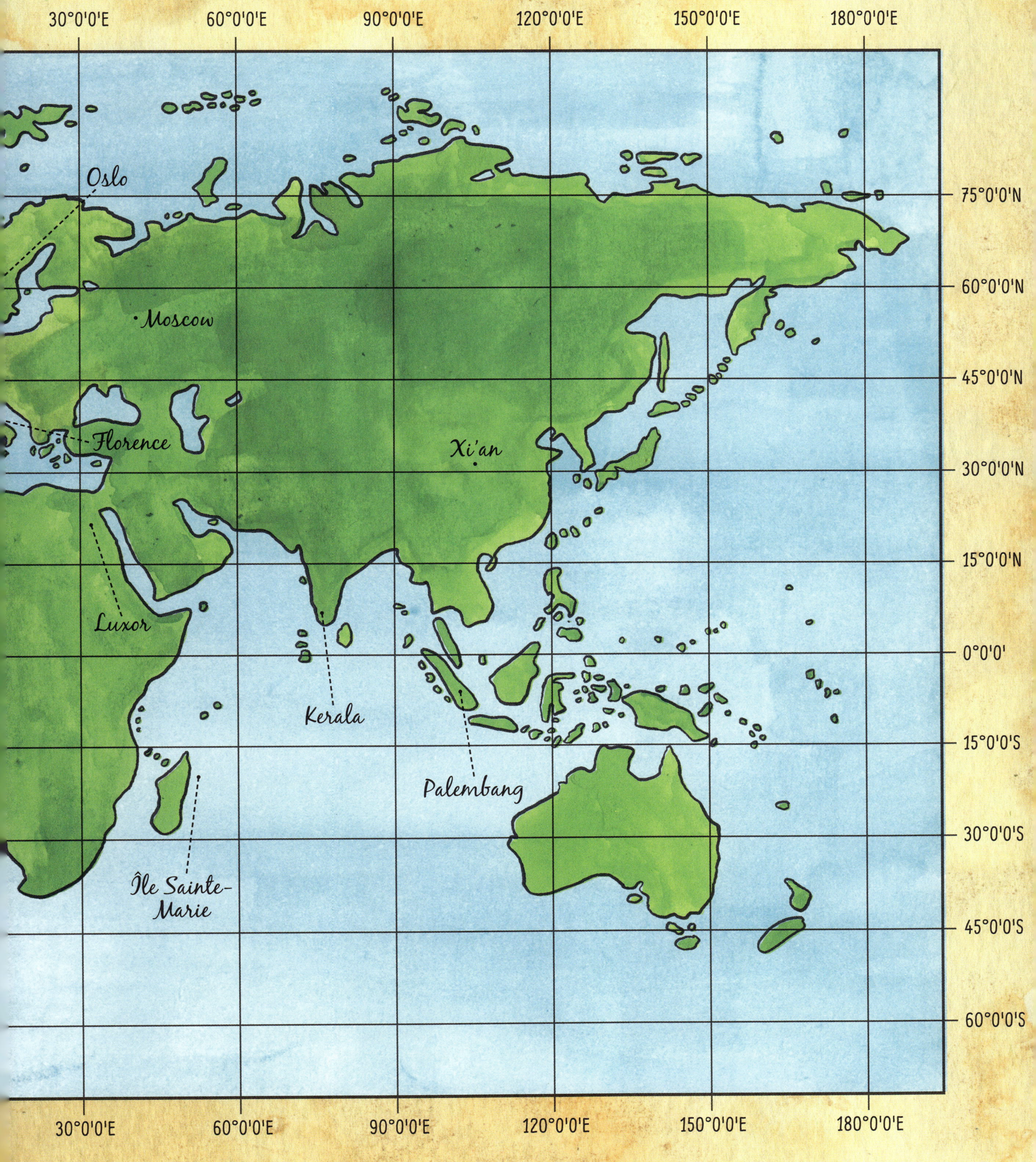
30°0'0'E
60°0'0'E
90°0'0'E
120°0'0'E
150°0'0'E
180°0'0'E
75°0'0'N
60°0'0'N
45°0'0'N
30°0'0'N
15°0'0'N
0°0'0'
15°0'0'S
30°0'0'S
45°0'0'S
60°0'0'S
Oslo
Moscow
Florence
Xi'an
Luxor
Kerala
Palembang
Île Sainte-
Marie
30°0'0'E
60°0'0'E
90°0'0'E
120°0'0'E
150°0'0'E
180°0'0'E

WHY NOT GO ON YOUR OWN TREASURE HUNT?

Orienteering

It's like a cross-country race, where you use a detailed map and a compass to find coloured flags called checkpoints. There's no set route. It's up to you to decide the best way to go so that you can tick off all the checkpoints before anyone else! Why not try contacting your local orienteering club to give it a go?

Metal detecting

A metal detector looks a bit like a broom, but instead of bristles it has a circular head at the end of its handle. Inside the head is a coil of metal. The metal detector works by sending electricity into this coil, which creates a magnetic field all around it. As you sweep the head above the ground, the magnetic field moves too. If there's a metal object nearby, it will become energised and make the detector go beep! You've just found treasure. It's probably a fork, but just think, it could be Viking coins!

Geocaching

This is the world's biggest treasure hunt. More than three million geocaches (small, waterproof treasure boxes in different shapes and sizes) are hidden outdoors in over 190 countries. Inside are treasures — trinkets left by other geocachers. All you need to do is download the app and follow the map to navigate to the cache. When you find it, sign the logbook inside and then trade one of the trinkets with something you've brought from home. Find out more at geocaching.com.

Nature's treasures

Look closely at the world around you and you'll find all sorts of natural treasures, from spotting rare wildlife on migration to finding fossils that provide a glimpse into Earth's past.